HOW TO GROW
HERBS

HOW TO GROW
HERBS

A PRACTICAL GUIDE TO GROWING 18 ESSENTIAL CULINARY HERBS, WITH STEP-BY-STEP TECHNIQUES AND 200 PHOTOGRAPHS

RICHARD BIRD

This edition is published by Southwater,
an imprint of Anness Publishing Ltd,
Hermes House, 88–89 Blackfriars Road,
London SE1 8HA;
tel. 020 7401 2077; fax 020 7633 9499

www.southwaterbooks.com;
www.annesspublishing.com

If you like the images in this book and would
like to investigate using them for publishing,
promotions or advertising, please visit our
website www.practicalpictures.com for
more information.

UK agent: The Manning Partnership Ltd;
tel. 01225 478444; fax 01225 478440;
sales@manning-partnership.co.uk
UK distributor: Grantham Book Services Ltd;
tel. 01476 541080; fax 01476 541061;
orders@gbs.tbs-ltd.co.uk
North American agent/distributor:
National Book Network;
tel. 301 459 3366; fax 301 429 5746;
www.nbnbooks.com
Australian agent/distributor:
Pan Macmillan Australia;
tel. 1300 135 113; fax 1300 135 103;
customer.service@macmillan.com.au
New Zealand agent/distributor:
David Bateman Ltd;
tel. (09) 415 7664; fax (09) 415 889

Publisher: Joanna Lorenz
Managing Editor: Judith Simons
Project Editor: Felicity Forster
Editor: Lydia Darbyshire
Additional text: Jessica Houdret and Susie White
Photographers: Jonathan Buckley, John
  Freeman, Michelle Garrett, Andrea Jones,
  Debbie Patterson and Polly Wreford
Designer: Paul Calver
Editorial Reader: Jay Thundercliffe
Production Controller: Steve Lang

ETHICAL TRADING POLICY
Because of our ongoing ecological investment
programme, you, as our customer, can have
the pleasure and reassurance of knowing that
a tree is being cultivated on your behalf to
naturally replace the materials used to make
the book you are holding. For further
information about this scheme, go
to www.annesspublishing.com/trees

Previously published as *Growing Herbs*

PUBLISHER'S NOTE
Although the advice and information in this book
are believed to be accurate and true at the time of
going to press, neither the authors nor the publisher
can accept any legal responsibility or liability for
any errors or omissions that may be made.

Contents

Introduction

Herbs have been an important part of gardening for millennia, being grown in the ancient civilizations of China, India and Egypt. They were known to the ancient Greeks and Romans, and there are also references to their use in the Old Testament. Some of the first gardens, created in the Middle Ages, were herb gardens, and they were often associated with monasteries, where they were used for both their culinary and medicinal properties. Today, we no longer have to grow herbs to provide remedies for coughs and headaches, and few gardeners grow medicinal herbs for their own use.

Culinary herbs, on the other hand, are still widely grown and used, and many gardeners devote sections both large and small to their cultivation. Some gardeners choose simply to grow only those herbs that they actually use in cooking, such as mint and thyme, while others prefer to make a more comprehensive collection, which can become a feature in the garden. Whichever approach you adopt, there is a tremendous range of herbs to choose from.

GROWING HERBS

Herbs can be grown in several ways. For many people the traditional herb garden remains the best and only way to grow them, and with care it can become an attractive part of the larger garden, perhaps contained by a neat hedge of box or lavender. In a small garden it is more realistic to include herbs in the vegetable garden or to combine them with the plants in the ornamental beds and borders. Another possibility is to grow herbs in containers, which is often the ideal solution for many gardeners because they can be sited near the kitchen door or moved around the garden as they come into season.

BELOW This beautiful garden illustrates the broad varieties of texture and colour you can achieve with herb plantings.

HARVESTING HERBS

Picking the herbs you have grown is a continuous process rather than a single, annual event. Once established, most plants will grow strongly enough to allow plenty of repeat pickings, which generally encourage new growth in healthy, well-maintained herbs. Usually, the plant will be taken during the growing season, but a few herbs, such as thyme, rosemary and sage, can be picked lightly when they are dormant.

USING HERBS

For centuries herbs have been prized all over the world for their remarkable culinary qualities. Leaves, seeds and flowers each have their own distinct flavours that add colour, texture and vital flavour to food. They can be used as garnishes; as flavouring for meat and fish dishes; for soups, stews and casseroles; for oils and vinegars; in drinks; and in breads, cakes and confectionery.

The therapeutic properties of herbs are well known, and although gardeners are unlikely to make anything more than tisanes, infusions, tonics and salves, many herbs are grown commercially for use in a wide range of medicines. Toothpastes, cough medicines and indigestion remedies are a just a few of the thousands of preparations that could not be produced without essential herb oils.

RIGHT A freshly gathered harvest of garden herbs, ready to be preserved and stored in containers for future use.

Finally, of course, herbs are valued for their fragrance. Originally grown for strewing and carrying in posies to disguise the smell of poorly ventilated and insanitary rooms, today even people who do not have a garden are likely to keep a bowl of potpourri in their sitting room or scent their bed linen and clothes with lavender bags.

RIGHT Herbs can transform foods into something quite delicious and irresistible. Here, warm Italian-style bread has been flavoured with basil and rosemary.

types of
herbs

The word herb derives from the Latin word *herba*, which originally meant a green plant. Now, however, we generally use the word to describe a plant of which some part – stem, leaves, roots, flowers, fruit or seeds – is used for food, medicine, flavouring or perfume. Most of the herbs we grow in our gardens today are annuals or perennials, although trees and shrubs, which provide leaves, berries and bark, can also be included in the category. The selection that follows consists of the most popular herbs, with descriptions of each type and how it is used.

Chives *Allium schoenoprasum*

This low-growing, hardy perennial, with narrow, tubular, rather grass-like leaves, is one of the basic culinary herbs that few gardeners will want to be without. Not only are chives invaluable in the kitchen, but their attractive flowerheads are also a wonderful addition to the ornamental garden.

An important culinary herb, chives have a more subtle flavour than their larger cousins the onions. The chopped leaves, which may be used as a flavouring or garnish, can be added to a wide range of dishes,

chives

including salads, soups and sauces, and they are frequently used to accompany egg and potato dishes. The flowerheads, but not the flower stalks, are also edible and can be added as a garnish to salads. Because they are milder than other members of the onion family, chives are rarely used medicinally, although they do act as a stimulant and digestive. They contain carotene and vitamin C.

Chives can be easily grown in the flower border and are excellent additions to a potager or decorative kitchen garden. They are also neat enough to use as an edging to a path or plot. The flowerheads of the species are pale purple to pink. There is an attractive white form.

BELOW Use only the leaves of chives because the flower stalks are usually too tough for culinary use.

ABOVE The naturally occurring white-flowered form of chive is usually grown for decorative purposes.

CUTTING CHIVES

Hold a bunch of chives in your hand, snip the bunch level at one end with kitchen scissors, then snip off the amount you require.

Cut straight across to form rings, or obliquely to form slanting chives.

Dill *Anethum graveolens*

A graceful, upright herb, growing to about 60cm/24in tall, dill is superficially similar to fennel, with which it will cross-pollinate. It has feathery, blue-green leaves and in summer bears small, open umbels of creamy-yellow flowers. These are followed by oval, brownish seeds, strictly fruits, which are strongly aromatic. Often seen growing as a weed on waste ground, dill is easy to cultivate in the herb garden.

Chopped sprigs of dill are, perhaps, most familiar as an ingredient in gravlax

dill with flowers

or gravadlax (dry-cured salmon), but both the leaves and seeds are widely used as flavourings, especially in Scandinavian dishes. They are also used with eggs, seafood, potatoes and fish. The seeds can also be included in pickles and chutneys. The taste is more subtle and less strongly aniseed than fennel. Essential oil is extracted from both the seeds and, to a lesser extent, the leaves and is used to make dill water, which is used to relieve digestive problems, especially of infants.

Because it is widely regarded as a weed, dill has not been widely hybridized. The cultivar 'Bouquet', which grows to about 90cm/36in tall, produces masses of seeds. 'Fern Leaved' (sometimes sold as 'Fernleaf') has beautiful dark blue-green leaves and is a good choice for a container.

In the Middle Ages dill was one of the herbs used in magicians' spells, and it was an important ingredient in charms against witchcraft.

BELOW The feathery leaves of dill are useful for decorating dishes as well as for enhancing flavour.

COOKING WITH DILL

To make a dill dressing, combine 6 large sprigs chopped fresh dill with 30ml/2 tbsp extra virgin olive oil, 15ml/1 tbsp white wine vinegar, 300ml/1¼ cups heavy cream and some pepper in a food processor.

To make dill vinegar, place 30ml/ 2 tbsp dill seeds in a small preserving jar. Top up with white wine vinegar and close the lid. Leave the vinegar in a cool, dark place for 2–3 weeks.

fresh dill leaves

Chervil *Anthriscus cerefolium*

With its delicately cut leaves and white flowers, chervil is increasingly being used in the kitchen for the subtle flavour of its leaves, which taste like a mixture of aniseed and parsley. Its dainty appearance as well as its flavour make it a valuable addition to a decorative herb garden.

Although it has mild digestive properties, and is sometimes taken as an infusion for this purpose, chervil's chief use is culinary. The delicate aniseed taste, which is more distinctive than parsley,

chervil

ABOVE Combined with parsley, tarragon and chives, chervil is an essential ingredient of *fines herbes*.

complements most dishes, and it is often added to salads, soups and *ravigote* sauces. It brings out the flavour of other herbs and is an essential ingredient, along with parsley, tarragon and chives, of the classic French combination, *fines herbes*. It is best used raw or in a very short cooking process, if the flavour is to be retained.

The most widely seen species, *Anthriscus sylvestris* (cow parsley, Queen Anne's lace), is often regarded as a weed, but the fresh young leaves can be added to salads. The cultivar *A. sylvestris* 'Ravenswing', which has purplish-brown leaves, is a striking addition to any garden.

MAKING *FINES HERBES*

The herbs needed to make the classic French combination of *fines herbes* are parsley, tarragon, chives and chervil. Discard any coarse stalks or damaged leaves from the herbs, then chop them very finely. *Fines herbes* can be used in marinades for fish, meat and poultry, in French herb butter, and they go very well with egg dishes.

French tarragon *Artemisia dracunculus*

A half-hardy perennial herb, French tarragon needs winter protection or to be replaced each year. It is grown for its narrow, strap-like leaves, and although it is not a particularly decorative herb, it is very valuable in the kitchen and is one of the basic herbs that should be grown. In hot, dry climates it produces loose clusters of yellow-white flowers.

French tarragon

French tarragon is used in salads, pâté, cooked meat, fish and egg dishes. Well known for its affinity with chicken, it also enhances the flavour of root vegetables. Vinegar flavoured with tarragon is a classic condiment, and it is a main ingredient of sauces and stuffings.

A larger and hardier plant, Russian tarragon (*Artemisia dracunculus* subsp. *dracunculoides*) has paler leaves and grows to about 1.5m/5ft tall. Its rather pungent flavour is widely thought to be inferior to that of French tarragon, although the leaves from mature shrubs are more palatable.

BELOW For the discerning cook, French tarragon is a necessity in any herb garden.

MAKING TARRAGON OIL AND VINEGAR

1 Collect tarragon in the morning after the dew has dried, but before the flavours have dissipated in the hot sun. Allow the moisture to dry completely before use, otherwise it may become mouldy.

2 Pour oil or vinegar into a wide-topped jar and add a large handful of tarragon.

3 Allow to steep for 2 weeks, then strain and decant into a bottle. Insert 2–3 long sprigs of fresh tarragon into the bottle.

Caraway *Carum carvi*

A biennial herb with feathery, bright green leaves, caraway has flat, cow-parsley-like heads of white flowers. It is grown for its seeds, which have a distinctive flavour that was first appreciated at least as long ago as the Stone Age. It has an aniseed taste and is used in a wide range of dishes as well as in breads and cakes. The leaves can also be used to impart the same flavour. It is not a particularly attractive plant but is important because of its seeds.

caraway seeds

Caraway seeds have been found during archaeological excavations at Neolithic sites in Europe, and the plant was well known to the Egyptians, Greeks and Romans. The seeds were a popular culinary flavouring in Tudor England, when they were cooked with fruit and baked in bread and cakes. They were made into sugared "comfits", and frequently served as a side dish with baked apples, as in Shakespeare's *Henry IV,* when Falstaff is invited to take "a pippin [apple] and a dish of carraways". This custom is said to have continued into the early 20th century at formal dinners of London livery companies. There is also an old superstition that caraway has retentive powers, and, if sprinkled about, is capable of preventing people and personal belongings from straying.

The seeds are used to flavour cakes, biscuits, bread, cheese, stewed fruit, baked apples, cabbage and meat dishes. They are also used as a pickling spice and to flavour Schnapps and the liqueur, Kümmel. The essential oil contains carvone and is used in perfumery and as a flavouring. Young leaves make a garnish and are added to salads. Seeds may also be chewed as breath sweeteners or as an aid to indigestion.

ABOVE The delicate flowerheads of caraway soon give way to aromatic seeds.

RIGHT Young tender caraway leaves add flavour to salads.

Coriander *Coriandrum sativum*

This herb imparts a distinctive flavour to dishes and so has an important role in the kitchen. It has enjoyed something of a revival of interest in recent years, and it is now one of the most popular herbs for use in both the home and in restaurants. Coriander (cilantro) used to be grown mainly for its seeds (fruit), but the lower leaves have become popular in a wide range of dishes and as a garnish, and some cooks use it in much the same way they do parsley, putting it in nearly every dish.

coriander (cilantro) plant

However, the strong, distinctive flavour is not to everyone's taste, and it is advisable to check that you really do like it before growing it in any quantity.

This is one of the earliest recorded herbs, and references occur in ancient Sanskrit and in Greek and Roman texts. Some seeds were even found in the tomb of the Egyptian pharaoh Rameses II, and the leaves are still put into soups in Egypt. The ancient Chinese believed that the seeds would confer immortality on those who ate them.

The leaves (which are sometimes known as Chinese parsley) and shoots are added to salads, soups and stews, particularly in India, China and South America. The seeds are a stimulant and digestive; they are frequently ground and incorporated into curries and meat dishes, as well as being included in breads, confectionery and liqueurs. The essential oil that is derived from the seeds is often added to massage oils, and it has a sweet, spicy aroma, quite unlike the plants, but its main effects are on the digestive system, and it is an important ingredient in digestive tonics.

LEFT The larger lower leaves of coriander (cilantro) are the most popular part of the plant.

coriander (cilantro) leaves

REMOVING STALKS AND FREEZING CORIANDER

To remove coriander (cilantro) stalks, pinch off the upper leaves, so that a minimum amount of stalk is still attached. Then pinch off the pair of leaves that grows further down the stalk. Discard the tough stalks. Wash the leaves and dry in a salad spinner, on kitchen paper or in a clean dish towel.

To freeze coriander, finely chop a generous amount of fresh coriander and place in ice-cube trays. The frozen cubes can be added directly to cooked dishes. Don't use as a garnish – once defrosted, the texture deteriorates.

Fennel *Foeniculum vulgare*

Widely used as a culinary herb, fennel is an extremely decorative plant and is certainly one to include in a potager or ornamental kitchen garden. The leaves of fennel are very finely cut and in some varieties they are bronze in colour. The tiny golden-yellow flowers are held in flat heads, from which are produced seeds that can be used in fish dishes and in sauces. The leaves can also be used in fish and other dishes. The flavour is predominantly of aniseed.

In the south of France, fennel is the perennial substitute for the annual dill, more commonly grown in the north. The foliage of bronze

Florence fennel

and green fennel decorates the garden as well as providing stalks – dried – to scent the fire for grilled fish, and fragrant green stuffing for oily fish. The leaves can also be used for fish stews. Seeds add flavour to stir-fry and rice dishes. The bulbous stems of fennel are eaten raw in salads or cooked as a vegetable.

fennel flowerheads

BELOW Florence fennel (*Foeniculum vulgare* var. *dulce*) is grown for the bulbous swellings at the base of the leaf stalks, which can be eaten raw or cooked.

PREPARING FENNEL SEEDS

Dry-frying and crushing fennel seeds before using them heightens and enhances the flavour.

Dry-fry the seeds first in a heavy pan for 1–2 minutes until they release their aroma, then crush the seeds in a mortar with a pestle.

ABOVE There are several forms of bronze fennel, which have copper or bronze-purple plumes of feathery foliage.

Bay *Laurus nobilis*

One of the most consistently used herbs, bay can be added to an enormous number of dishes, and the leaves are one of the key ingredients of the traditional bouquet garni. Surprisingly, however, few gardeners grow it, and most cooks use old leaves from a jar, which inevitably have lost much of their vitality. They taste rather bitter when first picked but are at their best and sweetest within a few days of drying. As a decorative plant it has much to recommend it, either in the herb garden or potager or as a container plant on a patio. It is a bush that will, in time, grow into a small tree. The leaves,

fresh bay leaves

dried bay leaves

which are the part used in cooking, are tough and leathery.

A first-rate culinary herb, a bay leaf is always included in a bouquet garni, and adds flavour to marinades, casseroles, stews, soups and dishes requiring a long cooking time. Bay leaves are also used to flavour sweet sauces and as a garnish for citrus sorbets.

Bay is an important source of the volatile oil cineole, which is lost from leaves that have been kept for more than about a year. The essential oil, which also contains geraniol, is used commercially to flavour condiments and liqueurs. The purplish-black berries are pressed to give an oil that is used in perfumery and in a number of veterinary products.

ABOVE The evergreen bay is a popular container shrub for formal situations, as here where a pyramid-trained specimen stands sentinel in a painted Versailles-style planter.

MAKING BAY KEBABS

Bay leaves add a warm, pungent flavour to grilled or barbecued kebabs. Push one or two leaves on to skewers, between chunks of meat and vegetables.

ABOVE Bay leaves dry very readily, retaining their shape well.

RIGHT Bay tree leaves might not look appetizing but, once dried, they add a sweet flavour to food.

Lavender *Lavandula* species

One of the most popular of garden plants, it is often forgotten that lavender is, in fact, a herb, originally used for strewing or for burning to improve the smell of rooms. Most of the lavenders grown today are cultivars or hybridized forms, and they form three main groups: *Lavandula angustifolia*, *L. × intermedia* and *L. stoechas*.

Among the most popular lavenders are those developed from *L. angustifolia*. They are neat, rather stocky plants with one sweetly fragrant flower spike on each stem. In addition to blue-grey, there are now forms with white, pink and purple flowers.

Lavandula stoechas

Another important group of lavenders has been developed from the hybrid *L. × intermedia* (a cross between *L. angustifolia* and *L. latifolia*), and these are known as English lavender or lavandin.

The third group is derived from *L. stoechas*, and they are easily recognizable from the flamboyant, butterfly-like bracts on top of the flowerheads. Some forms of the species have pretty, fern-like leaves. Abundant in the wild in the Iles d'Hyères off the French Riviera, this type of lavender is sometimes known as French lavender or Spanish lavender, and it is almost certainly the type that the ancient Romans would have recognized. Unfortunately, these lavenders are not reliably hardy and need winter protection in gardens that are subject to frosts.

Best known for the fragrant flowers, lavender is an important ingredient in perfumery, and the flowers are often dried for use in potpourri or for scenting clothes and bed linen. The essential oil, which has calming and soothing properties, is used in massage blends, bath oils, compresses, steam inhalations and also as a room fragrancer – its original use.

LEFT The compact *Lavandula angustifolia* 'Hidcote' has deep purple flowers and silver-grey foliage.

ABOVE *Lavandula × intermedia* 'Twickel Purple' has rich, purple flowers with a strong scent.

MAKING LAVENDER TISANE

Place 2–3 sprigs of lavender flowers in a glass cup and pour boiling water over. Allow to infuse for about 4 minutes before removing the lavender flowers. The tisane will have turned pale blue in colour, with an uplifting lavender scent.

Lemon balm *Melissa officinalis*

A perennial herb, lemon balm is widely grown but seemingly not much used in the kitchen. This is a pity, because its lemon-scented, mint-like leaves have a wide variety of uses in all manner of dishes and it is not usually available other than from the garden. One of its best known uses is as an infusion to make herb tea. It is an attractive plant for the first half of the year but looks rather ragged for the remainder of the year unless it is chopped to the ground so that it reshoots with fresh growth. The other advantage of doing this is to prevent it from self-sowing, which it does with abandon.

Lemon balm has sedative, relaxing, digestive properties, and infusions of fresh leaves are taken internally for nervous anxiety, depression, tension headaches and indigestion. It also has insect-repellent properties, is antiviral and antibacterial and is applied externally, in infusions,

lemon balm

RIGHT Lemon balm is a vigorous, bushy perennial, with leaves that smell strongly of lemon.

poultices or ointments, for sores, skin irritations, insect bites and stings. The essential oil is used in aromatherapy for anxiety states. Fresh leaves add lemon flavour to salads, soups, sauces, stuffings, poultry, game and fish dishes, desserts, cordials, liqueurs and wine cups.

In addition to the species, a number of cultivars with variegated foliage have been hybridized, making this a plant for ornamental beds and borders as much as the dedicated herb garden. *Melissa officinalis* 'All Gold', for example, is an excellent choice for semi-shade, where its bright golden-yellow foliage can be protected from scorching direct sun. 'Aurea' is similar to the species but has delightful yellow-splashed leaves.

MAKING LEMON BALM TEA

Lemon balm makes a zingy "tonic" tea and is a traditional antidepressant. For tea, always use the freshly gathered herb because both scent and therapeutic properties are lost when the leaves are dried and stored.

Put 30ml/2 tbsp fresh, washed lemon balm leaves into a pot containing 600ml/1 pint/2½ cups boiling water. Replace the lid to prevent dissipation of the flavours, and brew for 3–4 minutes.

BELOW The pretty golden-yellow leaves of *Melissa officinalis* 'All Gold' will shrivel and scorch in direct sun.

Mint *Mentha* species

Perhaps the best known and most widely grown of all herbs, mint is a genus (*Mentha*) comprising more than twenty species, and dozens of cultivars and hybrids have been developed, all with the distinctive flavour and aroma. There can be few gardeners and even fewer cooks who are not familiar with mint, and even someone who is not interested in gardening or cooking will recognize the taste from the spearmint in their toothpaste. There are one or two annual species, but most mints are perennials, with felty leaves and, usually, flowers in late summer to early autumn.

There is such a wide choice – probably more than could ever be used – that it is really a question of finding the two or three that you like and that suit your garden and growing those. The leaves of *Mentha × piperita* (peppermint), for example, are used in teas, iced drinks and scattered on salads, while those of *M. spicata* (spearmint) are used to make mint

ABOVE AND ABOVE RIGHT Many garden mints are so interbred that there are only marginal differences between them, as these two mints show. It is better to go by flavour rather than appearance.

jelly or sauce, the traditional accompaniment to roast lamb. *M. × gracilis* (gingermint) has a distinctively fruity aroma, which makes it an excellent accompaniment for melon and tomatoes. All mints are rich in essential oil, which is used in the commercial production of confectionery, liqueurs, toothpastes, deodorants, cough and cold medicines and indigestion tablets.

spearmint

peppermint

gingermint

MAKING MINT SAUCE

Strip a good-size handful of fresh mint leaves from the stems and chop the leaves very finely.

Pound the chopped leaves with 5–10ml/1–2 tsp sugar.

Stir in 30ml/2 tbsp boiling water. Add 30ml/2 tbsp vinegar and leave to stand for about 30 minutes.

Basil *Ocimum* species

sweet basil

No herb garden should be without basil. It is perhaps not as versatile as many other herbs, but when it is used, it is used to great effect. It is particularly good in association with tomatoes, salads (especially mozzarella cheese and tomato salad), and in a wide range of other Mediterranean dishes.

Several forms of basil are available, one of the commonest being the broad-leaved green basil, which has white flowers. Other forms include purple-leaved varieties, such as 'Purple Ruffles' and 'Dark Opal' which have small mauve-purple flowers, as well as sweet and lemon-flavoured varieties.

When cooking with basil, fresh leaves should be added towards the end of the cooking process so that its fragrance is not lost. Basil has an affinity with tomatoes and aubergines (eggplant) and adds fragrance to ratatouille, pasta sauces, pesto sauce and pizza toppings.

Basil flowers may be small but they have a beautifully aromatic flavour and are surprisingly sweet. To remove flowers from the stem, hold between your fingers and thumbs and pull – they will come away easily.

lemon basil

ABOVE Fresh basil flowers are delicious with salads, as pizza toppings or in tomato juice.

TEARING AND SHREDDING BASIL

Basil is best torn rather than chopped, since chopping tends to bruise the leaves and spoil the flavour. Tear the leaves into small pieces just before adding them to salads or dressings.

Basil leaves can be shredded into fine ribbons to make an attractive garnish for salads or soups. Stack 4–5 large leaves and roll them up tightly. Using a very sharp knife, shred the basil finely.

BELOW The green variety of basil is the most commonly grown.

BELOW Purple-leaved basil can be used decoratively in a potager or herb garden.

Marjoram and oregano *Origanum* species

Sweet marjoram (*Origanum majorana*), pot marjoram (*O. onites*) and oregano (*O. vulgare*) look similar but have slightly different tastes. Sweet marjoram, as the name suggests, is the sweetest, with a delicate flavour. Pot marjoram has a strong, even bitter, taste that withstands lengthy cooking. Oregano has a spicy flavour and is the most widely used in a range of dishes. Pot marjoram is probably the best for the ornamental garden, especially in its golden-leaved form.

marjoram

Many different marjorams are available but they will all enjoy well-drained, sunny conditions. The leaves are especially aromatic, and the flowers taste like a sweeter version of the foliage. They are a favourite of bees and butterflies and can be grown beside a sunny path in a cottage garden or among other herbs and roses. The golden-leaved or gold-tipped cultivars look particularly pleasing along the edge of a path.

In addition to its importance as a culinary herb, oregano is a valuable source of an essential oil used in food preparation, perfumery and liqueurs.

ABOVE Marjoram leaves give off a sweet fragrance when bruised.

oregano

BELOW Marjoram flowers can be infused to make herbal tea or preserved to flavour oils, vinegar and butter.

BELOW *Origanum vulgare* 'Country Cream' is very pretty but it needs protection from full sun.

Parsley *Petroselinum crispum*

Universally recognizable, parsley is probably the most widely used of all culinary herbs; indeed, some over-enthusiastic cooks throw a handful into nearly every dish or think it essential to adorn every slice of fish with a sprig or two. There are three main forms in addition to the type species, true parsley. *Petroselinum crispum* var. *neapolitanum* (otherwise known as flat-leaved or plain-leaved parsley) has a strong, distinctive flavour and flat, dark green leaves. It is this form that is recommended for adding to dishes to give extra flavour. Curly-leaved parsley, which is available as several cultivars, such as 'Moss Curled' or 'Super

curly-leaved parsley

Moss Curled', is a vigorous plant with dense, curled foliage, which can be used as both flavouring and garnish. *P. c.* var. *tuberosum* (Hamburg parsley, turnip-rooted parsley) has leaves with a celery-like flavour, but it is mostly grown for its root, which can be used in the same way as a turnip and is often added to casseroles.

Parsley leaves are frequently used as a garnish. They can also be added to salads, sauces, salad dressing, savoury butter, stuffings, meat, fish and vegetable dishes.

Fresh parsley is rich in vitamin C, and it also contains vitamins A, B1 and B2 and smaller quantities of calcium, protein and iron. It is a source of apigenin, which is an antioxidant that helps to reduce allergic responses. It is said that chewing a sprig of parsley will freshen the breath and help disguise the smell of both garlic

flat-leaved parsley

and alcohol. The essential oil is used commercially in food preparation and perfumery.

CHOPPING AND FREEZING PARSLEY

To chop parsley by hand, snip the leaves from the stalks and chop coarsely, bunching the leaves up against a knife. You can also use a herb mill or a coffee mill for small quantities of parsley, and a food processor for larger quantities.

To freeze parsley, wash fresh parsley sprigs and carefully shake them dry. Place in freezer bags, label and freeze. For chopped parsley, place in ice-cube trays and top up with water. The frozen cubes can be added directly to cooked dishes.

BELOW Curly-leaved parsley is used a great deal in cooking as well as for garnishing dishes.

BELOW Flat-leaved parsley has a stronger flavour than curly-leaved parsley and is becoming more popular.

Rosemary *Rosmarinus officinalis*

In the wild, rosemary grows as a semi-prostrate, rather sprawling, woody shrub on sand dunes as well as in scrub and woodland. Over the years the species has been hybridized, and there are now forms with more upright as well as more neatly spreading habits of growth as well as those with pink and white flowers in addition to the traditional blue. The cultivar 'Severn Sea' has bright blue flowers and a spreading habit, for example; the vigorous 'Miss Jessopp's Upright' is, as the name suggests, a more fastigiate form; plants in the Prostratus Group rarely exceed heights of 15cm/6in; and 'Roseus' has pink flowers.

Rosemary is widely used in cooking, especially in marinades for meat and fish, and it is an ideal accompaniment for courgettes (zucchini) and tomatoes. It is a classic partner, with garlic, for roast lamb and chicken. Sprigs of rosemary can also be used to flavour vinegars and oils. The essential oil is used in cosmetics and in some pharmaceutical preparations, including treatments for headaches and tension.

This is not only a herb for the kitchen garden, however. The needle-like leaves and attractive flowers make it one of those plants that it is almost impossible to resist touching to release the delicious fragrance every time you pass by.

ABOVE The best time for picking rosemary is before the flowers appear.

PREPARING ROSEMARY

Rub your fingers down the woody stem two or three times to strip off all the leaves.

Top chop the leaves very finely, using a very sharp knife with a curved blade or a mezzaluna.

Tender leaves from the tip of a young rosemary shoot can simply be snipped off with scissors.

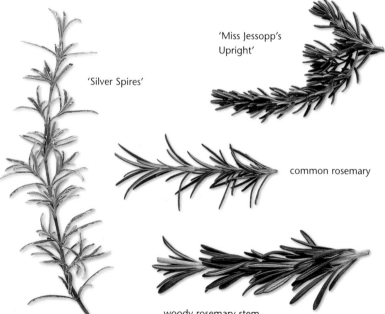

'Silver Spires'

'Miss Jessopp's Upright'

common rosemary

woody rosemary stem

Sage *Salvia officinalis*

The herb sage was originally native to Mediterranean countries, where it is found growing in scrub and stony pastures. It is an evergreen, rather shrubby and fairly long-lived perennial, with grey, felted leaves and spikes of blue-mauve flowers. Several named forms have been hybridized, including 'Purpurascens' (purple sage, red sage), which has purple-grey foliage, 'Icterina', which has yellow-variegated leaves, and the more tender 'Tricolor', which has grey-green leaves marked with cream, pink and purple.

Sage has a strong, distinctive flavour and is a popular culinary herb (the leaves of 'Icterina' are not as palatable as those of the species). Fresh or dried, the leaves are used in many Mediterranean dishes and with cheese, sausages, and goose, pork and other fatty meats. In Italy it is a traditional accompaniment for saltimbocca and liver, and it is combined with onion to make a classic stuffing for poultry. The essential oil is used commercially in the food and pharmaceutical industries.

Sage is an excellent decorative plant for the herb garden or potager as well as for ornamental beds and borders, where its evergreen leaves provide structure all year round. The late-spring flowers attract bees and other beneficial insects, making sage a valuable addition to organic and wildflower gardens.

sage

LEFT Sage bears decorative pink or mauve-blue flowers.

BELOW Sage has coarse-looking leaves that feel soft and felt-like to the touch.

Savory *Satureja hortensis* and *S. montana*

Although summer and winter savory are among the oldest of herbs, they are not widely grown or used today. Both are Mediterranean herbs that have strong antibacterial properties. However, the subtle, spicy flavour (like marjoram, with a hint of thyme) ensures that both summer and winter savory remain first and foremost culinary herbs.

Satureja hortensis, summer savory, is a small, bushy, half-hardy annual, to 38cm/15in high and with a spread of up to 75cm/30in. It has woody, much-branched stems and small, leathery, dark green, linear-lanceolate leaves. Tiny white or pale-lilac flowers appear in summer. *S. montana*, winter savory, is a clump-forming, hardy perennial, to 40cm/16in tall and spreading to 20cm/8in. It is semi-evergreen. It does not keep all its leaves in cool temperate regions through the winter, especially if frosts are prolonged. It has dark green, linear-lanceolate, pointed leaves and dense whorls of small white flowers in summer. It has a stronger, coarser fragrance than summer savory, due to the higher proportion of thymol it contains. There is also a prostrate white form, which is ideal for edging or a gravel garden.

The leaves of both species have a spicy, peppery flavour and are used in a wide range of vegetable dishes as well as in stuffings and other recipes. Summer savory has an affinity with beans, peas and lentils, and adds a spicy flavour to dried herb mixtures, stuffings, pulses, pâtés and meat dishes. Extracts and essential oils are used in commercial products in the food industry and in liqueurs, and in the pharmaceutical industry to make products for indigestion and sore throats.

ABOVE Winter savory loses its leaves during the winter, especially if there are long frosts.

winter savory

summer savory

LEFT Summer savory grows well in the Mediterranean and other warm and temperate regions.

Thyme *Thymus* species

This huge genus contains 350 species of evergreen perennials and subshrubs, all of which have small, aromatic leaves. In summer they produce little white, pink or purple flowers. Cultivars with variegated and golden foliage have been developed. There really is a thyme for every garden, and, as with mint, it is worth finding a few species or cultivars that you really like and planting them. Your choice is likely to be largely determined by appearance because, from a culinary point of view, there is little to choose among them, although the intensity varies widely, with the broader leaved plants having the strongest flavours.

Fresh or dried, thyme leaves are used as a flavouring in marinades, meat dishes, soups, stews and casseroles. All thymes are rich in the volatile oil, thymol, which has strong antiseptic properties. For best flavour, cut the leaves before the plants flower. The flowers themselves are attractive to honey bees and other beneficial insects.

thyme

RIGHT The commonest thyme is a bushy plant with small, lilac-coloured flowers.

BELOW Thymes are colourful plants with flowers in a wide variety of pinks, purples and white.

MAKING A BOUQUET GARNI

Thyme is an essential ingredient in the classic bouquet garni, together with parsley and bay. Take a sprig of thyme, some parsley stalks and a bay leaf and tie them firmly together with string. You could also include a piece of celery for poultry dishes, a rosemary sprig for lamb dishes, or a piece of fennel or leek or a strip of lemon zest to flavour fish dishes.

planning and
preparation

Herbs used to be grown in separate sections of the garden, and creating a small herb garden can make a delightful feature in a larger garden. Most often, however, reasons of space mean that herbs are grown among the vegetables or with other ornamental plants. Wherever you choose to grow herbs in your garden, give them the best possible conditions, and when it is necessary to replace a herb, it is a simple matter to propagate from seed or cuttings or by division so that you need never be without one of your favourites.

Where to plant herbs

Working out the design of a new herb garden is an exciting project, but before you begin there are several questions you need to answer to ensure that the end result is a success. Space is the first consideration. How much room are you prepared to devote to herbs? Do you have a large enough area to make a garden within a garden? Perhaps you would like to turn most, or all, of your existing space over to herbs? Or would a bed or border of herbs be more appropriate?

Plan how the design is going to fit in with your surroundings. Think about your house and current garden, because this will dictate the overall style you choose: formal, informal, old-fashioned or minimalist and state-of-the-art.

FORMAL GARDENS

Drawing their inspiration from the Renaissance gardens of Italy and France, formal gardens rely on geometric shapes, symmetry and balance to achieve their effect. Such schemes are usually designed around a central axis and often have a focal point, such as a statue or sundial. Paths of brick, stone, paving or gravel are laid in patterns and are used to impose the overall structure on the area. The plants may be contained in symmetrical sections within neatly clipped hedges, frequently of box or lavender. Formal gardens are ideal for herbs, which lend themselves perfectly to this type of layout, with conifers included to punctuate the planting and to provide height.

ABOVE Exuberant planting in a cottage garden style.

INFORMAL GARDENS

Designs based on fluid shapes and an irregular layout give plenty of scope for growing a wide range of herbs. They often fit better than formal schemes with the style of a contemporary house and its surroundings. Paths may be offset and gently curving, with beds and borders placed seemingly at random. Areas of hard material are often broken by greenery and flowers. Plants spill over on to the paths and spring up among the pea shingle; gaps left among the paving stones of a terrace can be filled with creeping, aromatic herbs. Bare expanses of gravel are not in keeping with this style of garden.

LEFT Neatly clipped box hedges associate well with herb gardens. They add order to what, at times, can be an untidy collection of herbs.

CONTAINERS

Growing herbs in containers has many advantages. Where space is limited there is always room for a few pots, even in the smallest of gardens. Sited near the house, they provide the added convenience of being handy for harvesting, which is important for culinary herbs, especially in wet weather or for a last-minute addition to a dish. As part of a garden scheme, containers can be placed in a bed to fill a temporary bare patch, used as focal points or arranged symmetrically to link different elements of a design.

Their mobility is a definite plus, but of course it must be borne in mind that very large pots will be too heavy to move. Unlike static planting in a bed, however, small and medium pots, or those made of a lighter material, can be moved around to make a change. This is also useful for plants past their best, which need a less prominent position in which to recuperate. Tender and half-hardy herbs in containers can be moved under cover for winter protection.

INDOOR HERB GARDENING

Some herbs adapt well to being grown as houseplants. In regions with cold winters that suffer from frosts, it is one way of cultivating tender herbs successfully. Give indoor plants as much natural light as possible and regular liquid feeds in summer, and do not overwater, especially in winter when light levels are low.

It is possible to grow herbs on the kitchen windowsill as long as you take into account the stress this puts on the plants. If you put a

ABOVE A selection of culinary herbs growing indoors in brightly painted tins.

young plant into a small pot and then keep cutting off its leaves, it will be hard pressed to survive. At the same time, it is being kept short of fresh air, the atmosphere may be too hot and steamy, and changes of temperature are extreme. From the point of view of flavour, there is little sunlight to bring out the essential oils.

The best way to counteract these problems is to alternate the pots kept on the windowsill with another set left standing outside. Keep the different herbs in small individual pots and group them together. They grow better in close proximity to one another because transpiration from the massed leaves increases the overall humidity.

Standing the pots on a tray filled with gravel or in a container with a layer of gravel on the base also helps to keep them cool and to retain moisture, without the plants becoming waterlogged.

LEFT Comfrey has deep roots and needs a tall container (left back). Marjoram (centre) and thyme thrive in smaller pots.

Planting outdoors

Most herbs will grow in the same soil you have in your vegetable garden, and, like vegetables, they prefer well-drained but moisture-retentive soil. Dig and prepare the ground thoroughly, adding plenty of well-rotted organic material. At the same time, remove any perennial weeds. This is particularly important around permanently planted herbs, such as chives, mint and sage, because there will not be another good opportunity to remove the weeds if they reappear.

PLANNING THE LAYOUT

Your choice of plants and the layout will be affected by the site. The type of soil, its drainage, the aspect, the amount of shelter and local weather patterns will be of paramount consideration. It always makes sense to work with the conditions and not against them, so a hot, dry, quickly draining site will suit Mediterranean herbs, while a heavy, moist soil will be better for plants that prefer streamsides and

meadows. Looking at how a plant thrives in its natural habitat will tell you how best to grow it.

Begin by making a plan, transferring scaled-down measurements of the area to be planted to graph paper. If you make several photocopies, you can scribble down ideas without worrying whether you are getting it right the first time. Make a note of vistas, established trees and lines of sight, especially views from windows.

FORMAL LAYOUTS

A formal herb design with a neat edging of box can look stunning from a first-floor window or balcony. Allow plenty of room for plants that spread, and bear in mind the eventual heights of the herbs.

When starting, prepare the site thoroughly, digging the soil well and raking it over. Transferring a design to the soil can be made simple by pouring sand out of a hole in the bottom of a container, thus indicating where the different

blocks of herbs go. If you make a mistake, it is easy to start again.

Thoroughly water all pot-grown plants several hours before planting, then knock them out of their pots by giving a sharp rap on the bottom of the container while holding the plant with the other hand. Firm the soil well around the roots after planting, water generously and label until you are quite sure of the names of the different herbs. A herb garden that is created from container-grown herbs can be planted at most times of the year, provided it is kept well watered, but early spring is the most sensible, giving the plants a full season to get established before the trials of winter.

SOWING

Some herbs, such as parsley, can be sown directly into the ground. This makes sense if you want to have a whole row or block of the same species. However, make sure that the soil is warm enough before

PLANTING A HERB

1 Using a trowel, dig a hole in the prepared ground that is slightly larger than the rootball of the plant.

2 Carefully insert the plant so that the top of the rootball is just below the surface of the soil.

3 Fill in the hole around the plant and firm down. Water the plant and the soil around the rootball.

1 Newly planted box trees line this wooden-edged herb bed and provide a framework inside which the herbs will be laid out. First, prepare the site by thoroughly weeding and forking over to break up the soil, then rake level. Dig in generous amounts of well-rotted compost or manure, and grit if necessary.

2 Deciding how much room to give each herb can be difficult for a beginner. Having consulted books as to the eventual spread of each, a helpful method is to outline areas on the soil with sand trickled out of a pot. If you make a mistake, it can be easily erased and begun again.

3 Remove the herbs from their pots and plant them carefully, with the soil fractionally above the level at which they were growing in the pot to allow for settlement. If you keep the pots for reuse, scrub them well with soap and water.

4 Water each plant thoroughly and keep them watered in dry weather until they are established. Avoid planting on a hot day when the plants will be under stress, and do not splash water on the leaves, which might scorch them.

you plant. In cold springs, wait until the soil warms up first, even if it means missing the theoretical first sowing date. Use a cloche to warm up the soil if you prefer. Parsley will not germinate if the soil is too cold, and you will have to re-sow because the first sowing of seeds will invariably rot. Thin the resulting seedlings to the appropriate distances.

For small quantities of herbs or in cold springs, it is a good idea to sow the herbs under glass and plant them out once they are big enough. They can be sown in modules to reduce the amount of root disturbance. Thoroughly harden off before planting out.

PLANTING

When you are planting out, remember that herbs need space to grow and you should allow for their increase in size. This is particularly important with shrubby plants, such as sage and rosemary, which can grow from small cuttings when first planted out to up to 1.2m/4ft or more across. In addition, when you are deciding what to plant where, put the taller ones on the sunnier side so that they do not overshadow the smaller ones.

Plant the herbs at the same depth in the soil that they were in their pots. Gently firm them in, water again and tidy up the soil to remove footprints. Loosen the soil if it is compacted.

Planting in containers

Containers are the perfect way to ensure that herbs are in just the right amount of light or shade. The mature herbs can later be planted out in the garden or kept conveniently close to hand in their pots on a patio or on a kitchen windowsill. Planting in pots also gives scope for adding height and depth to a border, and a group of pots can form an attractive garden or balcony feature.

CHOOSING POTS

Herbs can be grown in any form of container – even old coleslaw cartons, ice-cream cartons or plastic picnic boxes – but they will always look better and more at home if you choose an attractive container that has been properly designed for growing plants.

There are plenty to choose from – nurseries and garden centres stock them by the hundred – and they are no longer as expensive as they once were. Always try to choose one that is big enough for your needs. Remember that plants need room to spread out their roots if they are to grow well and remain healthy, and if you are intending to grow several different types of herb you will need one large pot or several smaller ones.

The shape does not matter too much as long as you do not choose an Ali Baba type pot, with a bulbous belly and a narrow neck, because the opening will not be large enough to get many herbs in (although such a pot could look beautiful with a single sage). Pot-bellied shapes work well if they are designed like strawberry pots, with openings in the side to take individual herbs. Window boxes also make good herb containers. They can be used on the ground or mounted outside the kitchen window or simply on a nearby wall.

Whatever type of container you choose, make certain that it has drainage holes in the bottom so that excess water can drain away.

BELOW Mints have vigorous roots, so it is a good idea to grow them in containers. Here, a selection of mints are growing in terracotta pots.

PLANTING

If the container is large it will be heavy once it is full of damp compost (soil mix), so, if possible, position it before you fill it. Cover the bottom of the container with irregularly shaped stones to help excess water drain away. Fill the pot with good quality compost and firm this down lightly. Plant the herbs, making sure that they are the same depth as they were in their original pots. Smooth over the top of the compost, removing or adding compost to bring it just below the rim of the container. Water thoroughly.

MAINTENANCE

The biggest task is to keep the herbs well-watered. In summer the container is likely to need watering at least once a day and even twice a day sometimes. All this watering means that nutrients quickly leach from the soil, so it will be necessary to add a liquid feed to the watering at least once a week. Alternatively, a slow-release fertilizer can be added to the potting compost.

REPOTTING

Container herbs will not last forever, and if you want a continuous supply it will be necessary to repot at least once a year. Many herbs are best thrown away and new ones planted in any case, and this applies even to perennials. Sage and rosemary will eventually get large, and it is better to replace these with new plants every other year, unless you have a container large enough to keep them for longer.

PLANTING HERBS IN A CONTAINER

1 To ensure that no stagnant water lies in the bottom of the container, place a layer of irregularly shaped stones in the bottom. This will ensure good drainage.

2 Fill the container with a good potting compost (soil mix). If you wish, mix in some grit to improve the drainage. Firm it down gently.

3 Plant by digging holes in the compost and firming the herbs in. Top up or reduce the amount of compost so that it is just below the rim of the container.

4 To ensure that the plants are kept fed, insert one or more fertilizer sticks into the compost, following the manufacturer's instructions on the packet.

5 Water the container thoroughly and place in the shade for a few days until the herbs have recovered and become established.

Stem cuttings

Propagating your own plants by taking cuttings is a rewarding and satisfying occupation, and it is by far the most economical way to replace plants and to stock your garden. The basic techniques are not difficult to grasp, but because the plants we loosely call herbs cover such a wide range of species, their requirements and the degree of difficulty in raising them varies.

TYPES OF CUTTING

There are several types of stem cutting, but the most frequently used are softwood, greenwood, semi-ripe and hardwood. The names refer to the time of year the cutting is taken and the state of the shoot from which the cutting material is taken. Softwood cuttings are taken from immature growth in early spring, usually from hardy herbaceous perennials. Greenwood cuttings are taken in early summer, just as the first spurt of growth begins to slow down. Semi-ripe cuttings are taken between mid- and late summer. Shrubs are usually propagated from semi-ripe cuttings, which need to be rooted in protected conditions, such as a cold frame or propagating case. Hardwood cuttings are taken in autumn, when stems have become woody and the leaves have fallen.

Some plants are best propagated by a single method, but some will grow from cuttings taken at different times. Lavender, for example, can be propagated from softwood cuttings taken in spring and from hardwood cuttings taken in early autumn. Rosemary, on the other hand, is usually propagated from semi-ripe cuttings taken in summer.

TAKING CUTTINGS

In spring, when herbs are growing strongly, take cuttings from the new season's growth. This is particularly appropriate for bushy herbs that cannot be propagated by division.

The cuttings should be inserted into a pot filled with damp proprietary cuttings compost (soil mix) or a mix of half sharp sand and half peat (or a peat substitute such as coir). Tap the pot on the workbench to remove air pockets. Use a dibber (or pencil) to make holes around the edge of the pot. You should get up to 10 cuttings in a 13cm/5in pot, but take care that the leaves do not touch each other. Water thoroughly. Place the pot in a propagator or cover it with a tented plastic bag. When the cuttings have rooted, pot up the cuttings into containers, using a potting compost.

TAKING SEMI-RIPE CUTTINGS

1 Choose a stem from the new growth of the plant (in this case artemisia). Cut it into sections about 15cm/6in long just below each leaf joint or node. Remove all but the top two or three leaves from each cutting.

2 Fill a pot with moist cuttings compost (soil mix). Dip the cuttings into hormone rooting powder and firm them into the compost around the edge of the pot. Cover with a plastic bag and place out of direct sunlight until rooted.

3 When a root system has developed and the cuttings have put on new growth (after 2–3 weeks) they can be planted out or potted up into larger pots. Artemisia becomes straggly after 4–5 years, but new plants strike easily.

Other types of cutting are taken in much the same way, but hardwood cuttings, which are really the simplest to prepare but take the longest time to root, are simply inserted into a prepared, V-shaped trench in a sheltered corner of the garden. Add some grit if your soil is heavy clay, insert the cuttings, tread in gently and leave until the following spring.

ROOTING OFFSETS

Some plants, such as chamomile (and strawberries), spread by sending out runners, which root wherever they touch the ground. So that you can control the spread of the plant and increase your own stocks, remove the offsets (offshoots) and pot them up individually until they have formed a good, strong root system (after 2–3 weeks) and can be planted out in the garden.

PROPAGATING SAGE CUTTINGS

1 Using secateurs (pruners) or a knife, take 13–15cm/5–6in long cuttings of the growing tips.

2 Trim each cutting just below a leaf joint. The secateurs must be sharp to get a good, clean cut.

3 Strip off the lower leaves, taking care not to damage the main stem. The leaves will rot if they are not removed.

4 Insert the cuttings into compost (soil mix) in polystyrene plug (divided) trays. Water and cover with a propagator lid.

POTTING CHAMOMILE OFFSETS

1 Carefully lift a chamomile plant and separate the satellite offsets (offshoots). It is important to make sure that each plantlet has part of the root system attached to it, so make sure you work with care.

2 Press each new chamomile plantlet into a pot of compost (soil mix). Water and leave in a shady place until new roots develop. It is important that you do not forget to water the pot, particularly during dry spells.

3 The cuttings will grow into bushy plants in 2–3 weeks, when they can be potted into larger pots or planted in the garden. This is the ideal way to produce enough plants for a chamomile lawn.

Root cuttings

Herbs with a creeping root system, such as mint, can be propagated by taking cuttings from the roots. Mint is particularly easy to propagate in this way because it has such invasive roots, and it is, in fact, best to grow mint either in containers or in sections of the garden where the root run can be restricted by paving stones sunk into the ground.

Root cuttings are usually taken in autumn or winter, during the plant's dormancy. Simply lift the plant, remove a section of root and, if you wish, replant the parent. The root you have removed can be further divided to create several new plants. Place the sections on the surface of a tray filled with moist compost (soil mix), cover them lightly with more compost, water and place in a cool but frost-free place.

Rather than propagating by taking root cuttings, it is possible to increase your stocks of fibrous-rooted plants or reinvigorate overgrown clumps by dividing them. Plants such as chives and marjoram, for example, can be lifted and divided in spring. The old clumps can be separated by hand. Make sure that each division has a good section of root or, in the case of chives, a new bulblet and replant directly into prepared soil in the garden or into individual pots so that they can be grown on for planting out later in the season.

ROOT CUTTINGS

1 Lift a root of mint and wash off the soil so that you can see what you are doing. Cut the root into 4cm/1½in pieces at each joint where you can see a small developing shoot.

2 Fill a seed tray with all-purpose compost (soil mix). Lay the pieces of root on the surface, press them in lightly and cover with a further layer of compost. Water well and leave in a shady place.

3 Once there are plenty of leaves showing, carefully separate the new plantlets and grow them on as individual plants in bigger pots or put them in the open ground.

DIVISION OF ROOTS

1 In spring dig up a clump of a perennial herb (these are chives) and divide it into several new pieces, pulling it apart with the aid of a small fork.

2 Firm each new piece into a pot filled with all-purpose compost (soil mix). Cut off some of the top-growth and water thoroughly.

3 Stand the pots in a cold greenhouse or sheltered corner of the garden. The new plants will soon grow strongly to provide plenty of fresh leaf.

Growing from seed

Many herbs are easy to grow from seed, and this is a good way to stock your garden inexpensively. Spring is generally the best time for sowing, although some hardy plants and biennials will grow from seed sown in autumn. There is no virtue in starting too early in spring when temperatures and light levels are low; seeds sown slightly later will produce stronger plants.

Seeds can be sown outdoors in spring but will be at the mercy of the weather and hungry birds. Sowing in seed trays, which can be kept under cover, is a surer way to success – especially for parsley, which needs heat for the seeds to germinate.

1 Fill a seed tray with soilless compost (growing medium). A tray divided into cells makes it easier to sow thinly and to pot up seedlings as they emerge. Water first, then scatter two or three seeds in each compartment.

2 Cover the tray with a thin layer of sieved compost. Never bury seeds too deeply, especially small ones, such as parsley. Water again very lightly and don't forget to label the tray (seedlings all look similar when they have just germinated).

3 Put a polythene (plastic) dome over the tray or enclose it in a plastic bag, to retain moisture. Put the tray on a windowsill or in the greenhouse and cover with black polythene or newspaper until the seedlings begin to show.

4 When the seedlings come through, remove the cover and put the tray in a light place but out of direct sunlight. Keep moist. As soon as the seedlings are large enough to handle, pot them up individually in 8cm/3in pots filled with potting compost.

5 Once the plants have put on some strong growth, they can be potted on into larger containers or planted out in the garden. Keep seedlings in well ventilated conditions so that they do not succumb to problems such as mildew and damping-off.

Harvesting and storing

Fresh herbs can be picked at any time during the growing season, whenever you need them, although obviously it makes sense to let young plants develop before harvesting them too much. Evergreens can be picked in winter, but only sparingly, as they will not be putting on new growth, nor will they have the same therapeutic properties while dormant as in the summer when the essential oil content is at its height. Herbs that die off or die back at the end of the growing season need to be harvested when at their best, then dried and stored for later use.

GATHERING

When harvesting for drying, pick flowers at their peak before they start to go over. Herbs required for their leaves should usually be picked before flowering. Snipping off flower-buds before they can form encourages a longer period of leafy growth. Shrubby and non-flowering herbs can be harvested at any time throughout the growing season.

Never cut herbs or flowers for drying on a wet day. The optimum time – though this is less important – is in the morning after the dew has evaporated but before the warmth of the sun has released too much of the essential oil.

DRYING

The secret of drying herbs is to remove the moisture without sacrificing too much of the essential oil content. This is achieved by drying at the correct temperature. A boiler room or airing-cupboard is ideal, but failing that, a warm, airy room is a good compromise. Even

ABOVE Harvest herbs when they are at their peak, usually before they flower. Cut them on a dry day, avoiding times when they are wilting in the heat.

a garden shed is suitable if it is completely dry. If possible, it is best to avoid drying herbs or flowers in direct sunlight.

Leafy herbs can be tied into little bunches and hung up, or they can be spread out in orange-boxes stacked on top of each other. Tie lavender stems in bunches to dry – it's a good idea to suspend them with the heads inside brown paper bags to exclude dust and catch any petals that drop. Spread flowers on tissue or newspaper, leaving them whole or twisting the petals off the heads. Leave herbs and flowers until papery dry to the touch. This can take up to a week.

LEFT Bunches of purple sage, rosemary and cotton lavender hanging to dry.

1 Pick seed just as it is ripening. At this stage it should readily come away from its stalks. Place it on a tray or muslin bag and leave the seed for a few days in a warm, dry place until it has dried.

2 Once herbs have been thoroughly dried, tip them into a glass jar with an airtight lid. Label the jar and store in a cool, dry, dark place.

3 An alternative to drying is to freeze herbs. They can be packed into bags and frozen, or finely chopped and placed in ice-cube trays. Add water to the trays and freeze to produce ready-to-use cubes.

FREEZING

A modern alternative to drying herbs is to freeze them. This has the advantage of keeping the plant's colour as well as being much quicker and easier to do. The cleaned herbs can be put into labelled polythene (plastic) bags and put directly into the freezer.

Alternatively, the herbs can be finely chopped and placed in ice-cube trays. Add a little water to each and freeze. Individual frozen cubes can be added to casseroles and soups as required.

STORING

Rub leafy herbs off their stems as soon as they are dry. The job is easier if you wear light cotton gloves.

Dried herbs deteriorate quickly if they are left out in the light and air. Keep them in a cool, dark place. Dark glass or pottery jars make the best containers. Herbs

RIGHT Freshly harvested herbs, ready for storing in a cool, dark place.

also keep well in sealed brown paper bags. This is particularly useful for heads of lavender.

Cellophane bags are fine for keeping herbs for short periods but don't use polythene bags or containers because they draw out residual moisture in the dried material. Dried herbs should not

be exposed to any dampness. If left in unsealed containers, they will take in moisture from the surrounding air and rot.

Although many dried herbs retain an aromatic scent for several years, for culinary and medicinal purposes it is best to replenish stocks every year.

Pests and diseases

Fortunately, herbs grown outside are generally free from pests and diseases. Buying strong, healthy plants in the first place, thinning out seedlings so that they are not overcrowded, and keeping plants well weeded are all ways of keeping potential problems at bay. There are, however, a few possible problems to look out for.

GREENHOUSE PESTS AND DISEASES

Herbs grown in the greenhouse may suffer from a variety of pests and diseases, which may occur whenever plants are cultivated in closed conditions. Check all plants regularly for infestation by pests; the presence of fine webs and damaged leaves may be the first sign of trouble.

If herbs are destined for cooking, it would be unwise to use chemical sprays, but there are biological controls available. These take the form of predatory insects, which can be released into the greenhouse, where they will attack the offending pest. It is now easy to order through the mail biological controls for red spider mite, whitefly, aphids, thrips and vine weevil, caterpillars and the scale insects that may attack bay trees.

Good hygiene in the greenhouse is important to help prevent diseases from gaining a foothold, and this involves clearing away any dead leaves and flowers, a thorough cleaning in winter and making sure that plants are adequately watered to keep them healthy. Keep the greenhouse well ventilated and use shading to control the temperature.

MINT RUST

Especially when grown in full sun, mint can develop a fungal infection known as mint rust. The leaves become covered in orange blotches, which eventually cause them to drop off. Fungal spores will then lie on the soil surface over winter.

Cut off and burn every emerging shoot for an entire growing season and cover the soil with straw in winter and then burn it. This kills the spores but does not damage the plant's roots. To avoid rust attack in the first place, grow mint out of direct sunlight.

LEFT Mildew is a fungal disease that grows on leaves. Keep plants in ventilated conditions to minimize the problem.

ABOVE Caterpillars cause damage to leaves, but removing them by hand usually keeps the problem within reasonable bounds.

SCORCHING

Golden-leaved plants grown in full sun may suffer scorching on their leaves. To control this problem, take care to grow certain herbs in semi-shade, in particular, golden marjoram, golden lemon balm and gingermint. Golden sage and golden thyme have thicker leaves and can stand more light.

MILDEW

Many herbs are susceptible to mildew, a fungal disease that causes a whitish, furry surface to appear on young leaves, shoots and flowers. It tends to be a problem in warm, dry weather, especially among plants that are growing too closely together. Pull up and burn affected annuals and dispose of the affected parts of perennials and shrubs. Water the soil around the plants and mulch well. Do not over-use nitrogenous fertilizers, which cause soft growth.

Growing herbs organically

As increasing numbers of people become concerned about the levels of artificial insecticides, fungicides and weedkillers used in the commercial production of all vegetables and fruit, the attractions of organically grown produce are becoming self-evident. Herbs are ideal for growing organically.

ORGANIC GARDENS

There is more to organic gardening than just not using chemicals. Organic gardeners work to improve the quality of the soil to provide plants with the best possible growing conditions. They also aim to develop a natural balance within the garden by attracting wildlife to help combat pests and to pollinate plants, and by growing a wide range of plants. In this way attacks by pests and diseases affect only a small proportion of the garden, and the inclusion of companion plants acts as a positive deterrent to some forms of pest.

GREEN MANURE

In addition to regular applications of well-rotted compost or manure, organic gardeners often sow green manures in ground that has become vacant as a crop is cleared after harvesting. These plants, which include alfalfa, some beans and peas and *Phacelia tanacetifolia*, are dug into the ground before they set seed and are valuable for fixing nitrogen in the soil.

BIOLOGICAL CONTROLS

Whenever predators appear, organic gardeners choose not to spray their plants with insecticides and other chemicals. Biological controls, which are increasingly widely available, are the ideal way of controlling many common pests. They usually work best when the weather is warm, although some are not suitable for outdoor use.

Introduce them as soon as the first signs of attack are noticed, and do not use any insecticides at all once a biological control has been introduced. Be patient and accept that there will be some damage before the biological agent takes effect. When you use biological controls there will always be some pests – they are essential for the predator to continue to breed – but the population will be reduced.

RIGHT Since herbs grown outside suffer from few pests and diseases, they are easy to grow organically. This way you can be sure they are healthy to eat, as well as having the best possible flavour.

cultivating
herbs

Herbs are among the most reliable and obliging of plants, growing in apparently poor soil and putting up with having leaves and flowers removed throughout the growing season. Many herbs will happily grow among your vegetables or in your flower beds, but to get the best from your herbs, however, it is worth spending time finding out which herbs are suitable for your particular location, climate and soil conditions. It is usually easier to fit the plant to the right environment rather than the other way about, as changing the soil and microclimate to accommodate a plant's preference can be difficult and costly.

Growing chives

Chives are easy to grow. Initially, you will need to buy – or be given – a plant, but once you have one you can go on dividing clumps as frequently as you like. Set the plants out in spring, planting them in a sunny position, in any well-drained, fertile soil, at intervals of 23cm/9in. You can sow seed in spring where you want the plants to grow.

If the initial clump is large, split it up and plant out the divisions as separate bulbs or in small clumps.

Every two years, divide the clumps to prevent them from becoming congested. Harvest by cutting off the leaves at the base. The flower stems are tough and should be discarded, although the flowers themselves are edible. Chives are best used fresh, but the

CULTIVATION

Planting time: spring
Planting distance: 23cm/9in
Harvesting: any time the plant is
    in growth
Storage: frozen or dried

leaves can be frozen, either individually or in ice cubes, or dried.

DIVIDING A CLUMP OF CHIVES

1 Although herbaceous herbs are traditionally divided in winter, chives can be split during the growing season. Dig up a clump of healthy chives, having first prepared a new piece of ground.

2 Use scissors or a sharp knife to cut the tops down to a few centimetres to make them easier to handle and because the leaves would otherwise quickly wilt.

3 It is now easy to pull the clump apart just using your hands. If the roots are very congested, use a hand fork to force the clump into sections. Alternatively, cut into sections with a sharp knife.

4 All these smaller clumps, each with about ten stems, have been produced from a single good-sized clump of chives.

5 Replant the new clumps of chives in fertile soil with a gap of 23cm/9in between plants. Water well and they will quickly regrow.

6 Lift and divide chives every two or so years according to growth. Pot up in good-quality compost (soil mix) in autumn for forcing winter supplies indoors.

Growing dill

Because dill is an annual it has to be grown from seed each year. Dill grows best in an open position and rich soil. Although plants will do best in full sun, in very hot areas provide some shade from the afternoon sun. It is advisable to avoid planting dill near fennel if you are planning to use the seeds of either plant, either for cooking or for propagation, because the two herbs can cross-pollinate easily.

Sow in shallow drills, 1cm/½in deep, in spring or early summer. Thin the resulting seedlings to 23cm/9in apart. Keep watered so that the growth is not checked, or the plants will prematurely run to seed. Start picking the feathery leaves when the plants are 10cm/4in high and continue to

do so until flowers appear. Harvest the seeds when they are ripe – that is, when they turn brown. The leaves are best used fresh but can be dried. Seeds can be dried and stored.

BELOW Grow dill in a sunny, well-drained site, either in containers or in ordinary garden soil. You may need supports as the stems can be rather floppy.

CULTIVATION

Sowing time: spring to early
  summer
Sowing depth: 1cm/½in
Thinning distance: 23cm/9in
Harvesting (leaves): late spring
  until flowering
Harvesting (seed): when ripe
Storage (leaves): dried
Storage (seed): dried

BELOW Do not plant dill near to fennel. The flavour of both plants will be impaired by cross-pollination.

Growing chervil

Although it is classified as a biennial, chervil is generally grown and treated as an annual, because the finely cut, aniseed-flavoured leaves, for which it is grown, are primarily used in the plant's first year. Unlike many other herbs, which do best in a sunny position

LEFT Chervil likes rich, moist soil in a partially shaded position.

BELOW Chervil leaves should be harvested before flowering, when the plants are still young.

in very well-drained soil, chervil is a cool weather plant – that is, it grows best when the seed is sown in early spring or, for a winter crop, in autumn. If it is grown during the hottest days of summer the delicate leaves burn and turn pink, and there is also a danger that the hot midday sun will cause plants to run to seed prematurely.

For best results the seed should be sown successively, at intervals of two or three weeks, starting in early spring. Choose a position in

CULTIVATION

Sowing time: spring or autumn
Sowing depth: 1cm/½in
Thinning distance: 20cm/8in
Harvesting: late spring or winter
Storage: dried

partial shade so that the leaves will be protected from the heat of the direct summer sun. Because chervil does not respond well to having its roots disturbed, seed should be sown in situ in drills about 1cm/½in deep. Before planting, dig in plenty of well-rotted garden compost or manure to the soil to enrich it and to enhance its water-retaining properties. Thin the emerging seedlings to about 20cm/8in and water regularly, which will also help to prevent plants from running to seed. Plants are hardy, but if you are sowing seed in autumn for a winter crop you will have to be prepared to protect the plants with a cloche or cold frame in gardens where the temperature is likely to fall below about 7°C/45°F for more than a short time.

The leaves should be ready for harvesting anything from six to eight weeks after sowing. If plants are cut back before they flower, they will produce a second flush of foliage. If it is left to go to seed, chervil will self-seed happily, and seed can be saved for sowing the following year.

Young plants are susceptible to damage by slugs and snails, and caterpillars can also be a problem.

Growing French tarragon

French tarragon cannot be grown from seed, and you need to begin by obtaining a specimen of this hardy, rather shrubby perennial. Make sure that you do not inadvertently buy a plant of the inferior subspecies, Russian tarragon, which may be sold instead of the true species.

Propagation is generally by means of root division in spring or by heel cutting in early summer. Plant the tarragon in spring in a sunny position in well-drained soil into which plenty of well-rotted garden compost or manure has been dug. Plants eventually grow to about 1.2m/4ft tall, but they tend to be fairly upright, so if you have more than one, they should be about 30cm/12in apart.

In cold gardens it may be necessary to protect plants when spells of freezing weather are forecast.

The seed that is sold is usually of Russian tarragon (*Artemisia dracunculus* subsp. *dracunculoides*), which is much hardier but has a more bitter taste. Russian tarragon is, in fact, often grown as a substitute for French tarragon, in spite of its inferior taste. It can tolerate much lower temperatures than the French variety.

CULTIVATION

Planting time: spring
Planting distance: 30cm/12in
Harvesting: any time
Storage: dried or frozen

BELOW The perennial French tarragon can be grown indoors in a window box filled with separate pots of mixed herbs. In this container (from left to right) are chives, flat-leaved parsley, mint, French tarragon, and green and purple basil. As a plant goes over, the pot can be replaced.

GROWING FRENCH TARRAGON IN A BASKET

ABOVE A perennial with branched stems and slim leaves, French tarragon prefers a moist but well-drained soil and full sun, and in cold climates needs winter protection.

1 Line a basket with moss and fill with compost (soil mix). Mix a teaspoon of slow-release plant food granules into the top. Plant some tarragon.

2 The finished hanging basket contains parsley, basil, rosemary and sage in addition to the French tarragon. Pinch out the growing tips to keep plants small.

Growing caraway

Caraway is a rather sprawling, inelegant plant, growing to about 60cm/24in tall and to 30cm/12in across, and for this reason it is best grown in a herb garden or wildflower garden rather than in a decorative bed or border. Native to western Asia, it is completely hardy and has become naturalized throughout Europe and northern parts of the USA.

A biennial, caraway is grown from seed, which should be sown where the plants can occupy the ground for two consecutive years because they will not flower and set seed until the second year. Caraway that is left to set seed will provide a succession of plants, and if you leave seed on one or two plants when harvesting, it will provide enough plantlets for the following year.

Sow the seed in a sunny position. Caraway is not demanding about the type of soil, but it must be free draining, and, because plants form taproots, it must be fairly deep. Plants do not transplant well, so sow the seed in situ from late spring to late summer in drills about 1cm/½in deep. Thin the seedlings to about 20cm/8in apart. In cold areas, seed sown in spring will take two seasons to produce seeds that will ripen. Autumn-sown seed will provide a crop the following summer.

The leaves should be picked while they are still young and fresh and before flowering for use in salads and savoury dishes. The seeds are harvested as they ripen and turn brown; they should be dried before storage. The roots are occasionally boiled and used as a vegetable.

ABOVE Although caraway is is best known for its aniseed-flavoured seeds, the young leaves are also a delicious addition to salads and many other dishes.

LEFT Caraway prefers well-drained soil and a sunny position. Propagate from seed sown in spring, preferably in situ as it does not transplant well.

Growing coriander

A hardy annual, coriander (cilantro) has light green, cut leaves and airy clusters of white flowers. The plants, which are not particularly attractive, grow to about 70cm/28in tall and to 20cm/8in across, and they are usually grown in a herb garden or wildflower garden.

The seed, which can be sown in spring or autumn, should be planted in drills about 1cm/½in deep in a position in full sun. Before sowing, dig plenty of well-rotted garden compost or manure into the soil. Coriander will not do well in waterlogged soil, so if you have heavy clay in your garden, dig in plenty of grit before planting. Germination can be slow,

but once seedlings appear, thin to about 15cm/6in. Hot weather will encourage plants to run to seed. In cool areas coriander will benefit from being protected by a cloche or by being grown in a poly-tunnel. Seed sown in autumn will grow on as long as plants are protected from frost.

Cut the heads as the seed ripens and allow the seeds to dry. The lower leaves are now used more than the upper, more finely divided ones, but both can be harvested when young. The seeds should be dried before being stored. The leaves can be frozen.

Although they are largely trouble free, coriander plants occasionally succumb to fungal

wilt, for which there is no effective chemical control. Remove infected plants and burn or otherwise dispose of them. Do not grow coriander or other related plants in the same soil for four or five years.

Organic gardeners grow coriander because the flowers attract hoverflies, whose larvae prey on aphids..

CULTIVATION

Sowing time: spring or autumn
Sowing depth: 1cm/½in
Thinning distance: 15cm/6in
Harvesting (seed): when ripe
Harvesting (leaves): while young
Storage (seed): dried
Storage (leaves): frozen

ABOVE Coriander (cilantro) is a popular herb with a pungent taste. Its delicate flowers attract beneficial insects to the garden.

ABOVE The white flowers of the coriander (cilantro) plant are followed by ridged, spherical, pale-brown fruits (seeds).

Growing fennel

This hardy perennial likes a sunny position and a well-drained, rich soil, although it will grow in quite poor soil. It can be grown from seed, station sown in spring in 1cm/½in drills at intervals of 45cm/18in. One or two plants should be sufficient for most uses (unless it is being used as a vegetable as well). Harvest the young leaves as you need them and collect the seed when it ripens. Remove the seeding flowerheads if seeds are not required to stop it from self-sowing everywhere. It is important to bear in mind that some herbs, such as dill and coriander, will cross-pollinate with fennel, which affects the flavour of the seeds and any plants grown from these seeds.

CULTIVATION

Sowing time: spring
Sowing depth: 1cm/½in
Thinning and planting distance: 45cm/18in
Harvesting (seed): when ripe
Harvesting (leaves): while young
Storage (seed): dried
Storage (leaves): frozen

Foeniculum vulgare var. *dulce* (Florence fennel, finocchio, sweet fennel), which is the best type for use as a vegetable, needs more moisture-retentive soil than ordinary fennel. It is not hardy, and needs protection from frost.

Fennel flowers attract hoverflies, therefore this herb is very useful in the organic garden.

ABOVE The filigree foliage of fennel is an attractive addition to the herb garden or to an ornamental bed.

CUTTING BACK FENNEL

1 Unchecked, fennel will grow to head-height, become coarse in stem and leaf and produce seed. If it is cut back early, however, it will make plenty of young growth for cooking.

2 Using sharp secateurs (pruners), cut the stems down almost to ground level. The fronds can be cut at any time during the growing season but are most tender in spring.

3 The leaves that have been cut can be put in the freezer for later use. In autumn the roots of fennel can be lifted and dried for use in decoctions, although the seeds are more often used.

Growing bay

Bay trees can be very decorative plants, especially if they are trained and clipped. Rather than one large bush, several smaller ones, perhaps shaped, make good structural features in a herb garden. They can be grown in containers and, in cold climates, overwintered indoors. The simplest way of growing a bay tree is to buy a young plant. If you need further plants, then take semi-ripe cuttings in the summer. Plant the tree in a warm, sunny position in well-drained, rich soil, although bay will tolerate poor conditions. Trim with secateurs (pruners) to keep it to the size you want – it will grow to 4.6m/15ft or more in a sheltered spot. Pick leaves as needed and keep a supply of freshly dried leaves ready for use.

CULTIVATION

Planting time: spring
Planting distance: 1.2m/4ft or
  more
Harvesting: any time
Storage: dried

ABOVE The large leaves of bay trees need pruning with secateurs (pruners) to avoid leaving ugly wounds. Use the prunings as cuttings for drying.

ABOVE A bay tree in a pot makes a focal point in the herb garden.

POTTING BAY

1 Leafy bushes of bay are reliable in containers, but be sure to plant in pots of adequate size. One such as this will sustain growth for several years before it is too small.

2 While there is still room in the container, smaller herbs, such as parsley, thyme and marjoram, planted around the base will transform the pot into a miniature garden.

Growing lavender

Lavender is an extraordinarily versatile and resilient plant. Hailing from the heat and dust of the sun-drenched countries around the Mediterranean, and even the desert regions of Saudi Arabia, the Yemen and Ethiopia, it is truly surprising that it is also happy living in the damp northern climes of the British Isles and even Norway. The reason is that not all species are hardy in all climates. While some forms, native to hotter climes, cannot tolerate any frost, others, such as *Lavandula angustifolia*, are hardy and will survive through several degrees of frost.

Lavender needs light soil – preferably sand or gravel in a dry, open, sunny position with good drainage so the roots do not get waterlogged in winter. Provided the drainage is good, it will also flower well in semi-shade. Generally, lavender does not do well on acid

ABOVE Dry lavender by hanging the stems in a cool, airy place.

soils, preferring chalky (alkaline) ones. If your soil is acid, use lots of garden lime and add a top-dressing annually. If you live in a very heavy clay area, dig a deep hole, line it with shingle to help the drainage and then add sand to

CULTIVATION

Planting and transplanting time: spring
Planting distance: 60cm/24in or 30–45cm/12–18in for a hedge
Harvesting: when flowers are fully developed
Storage: dried

the soil when planting. A little manure added when planting will help to establish the shrubs, but do not add too much as this will only stimulate leaf growth and weaken the scent.

Plant lavenders where you will brush past them to release their fragrance. Space young plants 60cm/24in apart, or for a hedge, place them 30–45cm/12–18in apart. Cut back faded flower stems and shape up the bush in spring, but do not cut into the old wood, because it will not reshoot.

PROPAGATING LAVENDER

1 In autumn take 12.5cm/5in heel cuttings, pulling the small branch away from the main stem with a heel of woody growth attached. Dip the heel into hormone rooting powder (optional). Tap gently to remove excess powder.

2 Insert the cutting into a pot filled with gritty cuttings compost, covered with dry sand. Place in a shaded position or a cold greenhouse and mist daily. Keep in a protected area over the winter and plant out the next spring.

Growing lemon balm

As its name suggests, lemon balm has a distinctive citrus smell, and it is, therefore, an ideal herb for placing near a path or at the edge of a border, where you can run your fingers through the foliage as you pass. This hardy, upright perennial will grow to 90cm/3ft or more tall and spreads to 45cm/18in, so allow it plenty of room in the garden.

Lemon balm will grow in any well-drained soil, and the species needs a position in full sun. It will not survive waterlogged soil in winter, so if you have heavy clay soil, add plenty of grit to the planting hole. It will grow readily from seed, which should be sown in spring in drills 1cm/½in deep. Thin seedlings to 60cm/24in. Established plants can be divided in spring or autumn every four or five years, and it is also easy to propagate from cuttings. Lemon balm will self-seed if the flowers are left, but cutting back plants before they flower will encourage a second flush of young leaves.

The variegated forms do better in partial shade and reliably moist soil. Direct summer sun will scorch the delicate leaves of the cultivar 'All Gold'. Any shoots that develop with plain green leaves should be cut out completely or the plant will eventually revert.

Harvest the leaves while they are young for use in infusions. The dried leaves can be added to potpourri.

ABOVE A lemon balm plant ready for dividing and replanting.

LEFT Once lemon balm leaves begin to look tired, cut the plant to the ground to get a second flush of foliage.

Growing mint

Mints grow best in rich, damp soil and partial shade. Most do not come true from seed or are sterile hybrids.

Grow mint from an existing plant, either by buying or otherwise acquiring one, or by dividing or taking basal cuttings from an existing plant. Plant in sun or partial shade in any garden soil, but preferably a fertile one. The questing roots have a tendency to spread far and wide, and to prevent it from taking over the entire garden, you need to contain the roots somehow – planting in a large sunken bucket with no bottom is a possible solution. Another is to plant it where it is confined between two solid structures, such as a wall and a path. Pick the leaves while they are still young and fresh. They can be dried or frozen.

STEM CUTTINGS

1 From late spring through the summer, take tip cuttings of various types of mint. These are such vigorous plants that they will form what are known as adventitious roots without any compost (soil mix) in a few days.

2 Remove the lower leaves and insert the stems in water in a narrow-necked bottle. Put the bottle in a light but shaded position, inside or out, and keep the water level topped up. When the roots have formed, pot up individually into small 8cm/3in pots.

ABOVE Plants such as mint that spread rapidly underground should be planted in a large bucket or flowerpot, with plenty of drainage holes, which is then sunk into the ground. The rim of the pot should be level with the surface of the soil.

ROOT CUTTINGS

1 Mint beds need regular renewal, which is easily done by taking healthy young roots, trimming them into short sections and pressing these into trays of moist compost (soil mix).

2 Cover the cuttings with a layer of compost, and they will soon start to grow. Those prepared in early autumn can provide young shoots for winter use.

Growing basil

There are several species and hybridized forms of basil, but the basic type is *Ocimum basilicum*, often referred to as sweet basil. There is also a beautiful purple variety, *O. b.* var. *purpurascens*, but the flavour of the purple-leaved form is less strong than that of the green variety. *O. b.* 'Cinnamon' has distinctive cinnamon-flavoured foliage, and the hybrid basil *O. × citriodorum* has a strong citrus scent.

They are mostly half-hardy annuals and must be grown from seed each year. Basil can be grown in the open ground, but it is often more convenient to use containers. All basils like a warm, sunny position and a moist, fertile soil. Sow in trays in a gentle heat in early spring and plant out after the threat of frosts is over. It can also be sown directly in the soil in late spring, but the soil must be kept moist. Plant out or thin to intervals

CULTIVATION

Sowing time: spring
Sowing depth: 1cm/½in
Thinning and planting distance: 23cm/9in
Harvesting: any time
Storage: dried or frozen

of 23cm/9in. Pick the leaves as required. They are best used fresh but can be dried, frozen or puréed in a fusion of olive oil.

GROWING BASIL FROM SEED

1 Seeds may be sown individually in soil blocks to save pricking out later, or seedlings can be transferred from seed trays.

2 The rich compost mixture of the soil blocks combined with heat and regular watering encourages rapid early growth.

3 With two pairs of true leaves, these seedlings are well established and ready for potting up.

4 After hardening off, these young basil plants will soon be ready for transfer to the open garden.

Growing marjoram and oregano

Marjoram and oregano are native to the Mediterranean, where they are found growing in dry soils on sunny, open hillsides. All the marjorams and oreganos will do best if they are grown in full sun, preferably in a rich, well-drained soil. Plants grown in cooler, wetter regions do not have the same intensity of flavour as those grown in a Mediterranean climate.

Marjoram and oregano can be grown from seed sown in spring in shallow drills at a depth of 1cm/½in. Seed is slow to germinate. Existing plants can be divided in the spring. They should either be thinned or planted at intervals of 30cm/12in.

All the species are perennial, but sweet marjoram is more tender and may have to be re-sown each year or grown in a pot and taken indoors for the winter. Harvest the leaves while they are young. They can be dried or frozen for storage.

BELOW Oregano requires well-drained soil and a sunny position. *Origanum vulgare* is best propagated by division or by cuttings taken in summer.

HARVESTING MARJORAM

1 Marjoram is easily air dried. Cut bunches of healthy material at mid-morning on a dry, warm day. Strip off the lower leaves.

2 Twist a rubber band around the marjoram stems to hold them tightly together.

3 Gather as many bunches as you need, then place them in a dry, well-ventilated place where they are protected from light.

Growing parsley

All types of parsley are useful in the kitchen, but the curly-leaved forms are more attractive in the garden. Parsley does best in a sunny spot but will take light shade. Grow in a moist, fertile soil. Treat parsley as an annual, growing it from seed sown in spring to provide leaves for use during summer and autumn; a second sowing in late summer will give leaves for winter use.

Cover the winter crop with a cloche, partly to protect it and partly to prevent mud from being splashed on the leaves. Sow the seeds in 1cm/½in drills and thin to about 23cm/9in apart. Parsley is slow to germinate, especially if the soil is cold. Do not let the soil become too dry. Harvest the leaves as needed. Dry or freeze for storage.

ABOVE Parsley does best in rich, moisture-retentive soil in partial shade. Sun will encourage flowers to form.

RIGHT Cut down the flower stems of parsley as soon as they appear. This will encourage leaf growth.

CULTIVATION

Sowing time: spring or late summer
Sowing depth: 1cm/½in
Thinning distance: 23cm/9in
Harvesting: any time
Storage: dried or frozen

PLANTING PARSLEY IN A BASKET

1 Plant parsley into the sides of a basket, resting the rootballs on the compost (soil mix), feeding leaves through the wires.

2 Dwarf beans can be added to create a bushy, green display. Remove sprigs regularly to encourage new shoots.

Growing rosemary

Rosemary is one of those herbs that should be planted next to a path or patio so that you can appreciate its lovely scent as you pass by. However, rosemary can grow quite large, so do not plant it too close to the path or it will eventually cause an obstruction. If it is established in the right position, however, rosemary will grow for many years, although it may eventually get rather straggly. If you have limited space, choose 'Miss Jessopp's Upright', which has an upright habit.

Rosemary is marginally tender and may succumb to a very cold winter. It needs well-drained, alkaline soil and a warm, sunny position. It is best to start with a bought plant or one grown from cuttings. Plant out in spring, and if you need more than one plant set them 75cm/30in apart. Pick the leaves as required, but those that are needed for drying are best picked before the flowers appear.

CULTIVATION

Planting time: spring or late
   summer
Planting distance: 75cm/30in
Harvesting: any time
Storage: dried

LEFT If you want to topiarize rosemary, begin with a young plant and remove the lowest stems. As the tops grow, trim them to shape. This will probably be once in the second summer.

BELOW Rosemary forms a neat, evergreen hedge-like boundary in this enclosed herb garden. Trim the stems after flowering to maintain a tidy shape.

LAYERING

1 Choose a low, flexible branch, remove some of the leaves where it touches the soil and cut a shallow notch to induce rooting.

2 Scoop out a shallow depression or sink a pot in the ground for the prepared section of branch, and hold it in place with a wire loop or clothes peg.

3 Cover the wounded section and peg with good topsoil and firm gently. In dry weather, water the layer (but not the parent plant) to hasten rooting.

Growing sage

All forms of sage like a well-drained soil in a sunny position. Although *Salvia officinalis* is hardy, it does not always withstand prolonged cold below -10°C/14°F, especially in wet conditions. The cultivars are slightly less hardy than the species.

Sage is best grown from cuttings or purchased as young plants, although plants can also be grown from seed. They should be planted out in spring, and if several sage plants are required they should be planted 60cm/24in apart.

Prune sage in the spring to keep it in good shape, or just after flowering, but do not cut into the wood. After a few years, sages can become straggly and need to be replaced. Pineapple sage must be protected from frost and kept under cover during the winter. Grow in moist soil and if container-grown, keep the compost (soil mix) damp.

ABOVE Pruning sage each year ensures fresh, new growth. Eventually, the sage plants will get straggly and woody and should be replaced.

RIGHT Evergreen perennials such as sage can quickly develop into impressive mounds of shrubby growth.

Sage is easy to propagate from softwood cuttings taken throughout the summer. Leaves can be picked at any time, but those for drying are best picked before flowers appear.

CULTIVATION

Sowing time: spring
Sowing depth: 1cm/½in
Cuttings taken: summer
Planting distance: 60cm/24in
Harvesting: any time
Storage: dried

MOUNDING

1 When old woody herbs develop bare lower stems, they can be propagated by mounding.

2 Clear out any dead stems and leaves, and then heap soil in the centre of the bush.

3 Leave for a few months. Each of the branches will have rooted and can be detached as a new plant.

Growing savory

Both summer savory and winter savory are native to Mediterranean countries, but summer savory is a half-hardy annual, while winter savory is a hardy perennial.

Summer savory is usually grown from seed, sown in situ in spring in drills about 1cm/½in deep with the seeds set about 30cm/12in apart. Plants will grow in any soil as long as it drains freely, and if you garden on heavy clay, fork plenty of chippings into the ground before you begin.

Winter savory can also be easily grown from seed, which should be left on the surface of the soil and not buried. It does best in light, neutral to alkaline, well-drained soil in a sunny position. Plants can be grown from cuttings taken in summer and established plants can be divided in spring. Winter savory can also be propagated by layering, which is best attempted in spring. It will crop for most of the year, especially if it is grown in a pot that can be moved under cover in winter. Although it is a hardy plant, in gardens that are exposed to cold, drying winter winds and hard frosts, protect plants with a thick mulch and some horticultural fleece.

CULTIVATION

Sowing time: mid-spring
Sowing depth: 1cm/½in
Thinning distance: 30cm/12in
Harvesting: any time
Storage: dried

Several attractive cultivars of winter savory are available, including a prostrate white form and the more upright *Satureja montana* 'Purple Mountain'. Winter savory is useful in the organic garden because the flowers attract bees. Both types of savory enjoy the good drainage that is provided in raised beds.

ABOVE Summer savory has small, leathery, dark green leaves, which have a midly spicy flavour. Tiny white or pale lilac flowers appear in summer.

LEFT The leaves of both types of savory are best harvested just as the flowers begin to open. They can be used fresh or dried before being stored.

Growing thyme

Thymes are good plants for growing in the cracks and crevices between paving in the herb garden. Being robust plants, they can even survive being walked on – and it will make them release their wonderful fragrance. However, care should be taken if people are likely to walk over the thyme in bare feet, because the herbs are usually full of bees when in flower.

Thymes are easy to grow, but they do need replacing from time to time as they grow rather straggly and threadbare. They like a sunny position in light, sandy, well-drained soil. They can be grown from purchased plants or from cuttings taken at any time from existing plants. Set the plants about 30cm/12in apart and keep them well weeded. Trim over the more

CULTIVATION

Cuttings taken: any time
Planting distance: 30cm/12in
Harvesting: any time
Storage: dried

straggly forms after flowering to keep them more compact. Harvest the leaves as required. They can be dried for storage.

PLANTING A THYME POT

1 Place crocks over the drainage hole in the bottom of a herb pot. Put a layer of compost (soil mix) mixed with grit in the bottom of the pot until it reaches the level of the first hole.

2 Remove a thyme plant from its pot and shake off any excess compost. Gently feed it through one of the holes. Add compost, bedding the plant in well. Repeat with another thyme.

3 Finally, plant a 'Porlock' thyme in the top of the pot, add more compost around the edges, and bed it in firmly. Water well. Once planted, water when the top of the compost feels dry.

PLANTING A THYME SUNDIAL

1 Compact and low-growing thyme plants in a range of colours, forms and scents make a pretty composition in a container around a sundial. Add grit to the compost (soil mix) before planting.

2 After a few weeks the plants have grown to fill the pot and spill over the edges. Keep cutting the thymes so that an upright variety does not take over, and allow them to flower to add even more variety to the planting.

Index